Two Sides of the Door

Poems by
Esther Elizabeth

Cover photo by Esther Elizabeth
Layout design by Dale Stitt

Two Sides of the Door
Copyright © 2016 Esther Elizabeth

ISBN-10:0692671404
ISBN-13:978-0692671405

Two Sides of the Door

A note about the poems

People come into our lives all the time to teach us something we need to know about ourselves. I've made it my life's work to try and live awake, to open my heart and eyes to these teaching encounters. **Two Sides of the Door** is a collection of new and old poems that tell my stories of such moments. I bow in gratitude to the teachers I have met along the path.

To Billy and the many I've encountered on the journey that walk close to the edge and close to their deep heartbeat of truth.

Thank you to my husband Dale Stitt for being a grounded presence and first reader of each poem; Mia Nyschens for hours of volunteer editing; John Miller for proof editing; and Kim Stafford for unwavering support and kindness.

Appreciation There are few gifts greater than having people in our world who simply love us, believe in us, encourage the creative spirit in us. I have such people in my life and I'm immensely blessed, humbled, grateful. To each...thank you.

Table Of Contents

Winter Feet

Early morning walk
Down Broadway
Inner city sidewalk
Still dark
Still cold

Ezra, a man I've come to know
Sleeps in a doorway
His blue tennis shoes
neatly placed next to his head

His bare feet
Extend out from the heavy blanket

I walk on
Then turn around
Gently pull the blanket over his feet

Ezra whispers a sleepy *thank you*
I start to leave
He kicks the blanket off

Feet once again bare
To the bitter cold
Life as he lives it
Exposed

My First Poem – Ever

Thank you for writing poems about me, says Billy,
a homeless friend I meet up with most Thursdays
on the corner of 10th and Salmon.

Now I'd like to write a poem about you, he announced,
but I don't know how.

Poems are just a series of short lines, I say.
You write a poem one line at a time. I'll help you.

I take out my pen and notebook, and he begins.

My First Poem – Ever
That's the title, laughs Billy, clearly enjoying himself.

I have a friend. I met her a long time ago.
She is white. I am black.
She is some kind of spiritual, I am Muslim.
She writes poems about our times together.
Now I'm writing about her.

Billy stops, sips his coffee, leans his head back
and stares at the broken street light.

Are you finished? I inquire.
Keep writing, Billy says.

On those days we meet up,
I take a break from selling newspapers.
We sit, drink coffee, talk, eat the scones she brings.
She's a really good friend.

Billy stops. His eyes begin to water.
There is a long pause.

All my life I've wanted to be seen and heard.
That's what happens when we're together.
Now, I'm writing a poem, my first poem – ever.

We sit for a long time in silence,
taking in the magnitude of his comment.

I'm going to put this poem in my new book, I say.
Aware that I don't even know his last name,
I ask how I should sign his poem.

Just Billy. That's who I am. Just Billy.

Pink Bunny

Standing in line at a local coffee shop
a curly-headed young girl
in a yellow flowered dress
showed me the book *Pink Bunny*.

"Read," she said in her sweet soft voice.

Her mother, discussing the details
of a dinner party on her cell phone,
stopped long enough
to tell her daughter she
would read the book to her,
then returned to her phone conversation.

With coffee in hand and no empty chairs,
I sat on the floor next to the children's table
and the young girl in the yellow flowered dress.

"Read," she said again,
handing me *Pink Bunny*.
And so I did.
Twice.

The physically fit,
attractively dressed mother
finally ended her conversation
and apologized for her daughter,
"I don't know why,
but she can be such a pest – so persistent."

"She just wants to know about the pink bunny,"
I said, "and she knows you aren't serious
about reading it to her."

The little girl again handed me the book.
The mother grabbed it.
"I will read the book.
If anyone is going to read, it will be me."

Her cell phone rang.
She answered, and *Pink Bunny*
fell to the floor.

Lock of Hair

I rode my bike down the long dirt road
to visit the old woman
my mother told me never to visit.

"She is evil," said my mother.
"She holds secrets. Children who visit her disappear.
She is crazy in the head.
Don't ever go down that road."

I went down the long dusty dirt road
one hot summer day.
She sat on the porch of the broken-down farmhouse
as if expecting me.
This aged woman who made the village people
uncomfortable was not scary. She was soft-spoken,
kind, seasoned and beautiful.

She invited me to come and sit next to her
and have some lemonade.
Said her name was Idy Hicks,
used to be part of the Underground Railroad,
hid runaway slaves in the old cellar out back.

Later in the afternoon,
hours after I should have been home,
she promised me
if I would let her cut a lock of my hair,
I would have a long, meaningful, blessed life.
I would become a healer, a wise woman.

I let her cut my hair.

Saving Sally

I had been sober for two years
when Sally called.
I had been avoiding her.
Hanging out with old drinking buddies
was not part of my recovery program.

We met for brunch.
Sally had already been drinking.
She had to in order to keep away the shakes,
dry heaves, other symptoms of withdrawal
that start after only a day,
or even a few hours, without alcohol.

I was shocked
at how old and ashen she looked.
She knew she was in serious trouble,
said it was her choice to drink her way into death.

I decided to save Sally.

I felt responsible for her drinking,
for her life. Why?
Was it shame and guilt
for the times I encouraged her to drink with me,
for introducing her to gin and tonic,
her current drug of choice?
Was it arrogance
that I was finally sober and she wasn't?
Was I afraid
that if she did not stop drinking,
I would start again?
Did I fear how I would handle her dying?

Whatever the reasons,
I felt I owed it to Sally,
my recovery, our friendship,
to do everything I could to save her.

Saving Sally was hard work.
I organized an intervention
with her husband and son,
formed a support network,
located a detox center
that would admit her one more time.
I did everything right
according to the intervention handbook.
I was courageous, did not give up,
did not buckle anytime
I heard "fuck you."

Her husband called me daily
to find out what my next step was
after the last one failed.
He wanted to leave her, again;
but again I talked him into staying,
convinced we were making progress.

I brought the problem of Sally
to my 12-step meetings,
my sponsor, my therapist.
They all said the same thing:
I was not responsible
for her behavior
or her life.
By focusing on Sally,
I jeopardized my own recovery.

They were tired of hearing about her,
threatened to do an intervention on me
should my obsession with Sally continue.
I ignored their collective insight.

Sally became more and more belligerent,
more and more out of control,
and closer and closer
to dying of the disease
that was taking over her mind, body, soul.

I finally had to admit
that the greatest problem
with my plan to save Sally was –

Sally did not want to be saved.

A few months later
I delivered the eulogy at her funeral.

The Village Walker

She walked for hours
up one street, down another,
circling the village many times.

She walked fast with a steady gait,
hands swinging at her sides,
looking straight ahead, ignoring
men sitting outside Jake's Barbershop,
Beryl and Maple, the town socialites
and gossipmongers,
and others seeking to get her attention.

The village people mocked
the way she walked,
made fun of her oversized earrings,
the bright red lipstick
that altered the shape of her mouth,
called her eccentric,
an oddity, a recluse.

One day my friend Jenny and I
decided to follow her,
learn her route,
see what she saw on her walks.

We watched her slender hips
and gypsy skirt swinging
back and forth
sharing the same rhythm as her long
wavy dyed-red hair.

We couldn't keep up.
She quickly disappeared,
leaving us sitting on the curb
at the corner of Main and Elliot.

I moved away from the village
but happened to be home
the Friday she died.

There was no service, only a one-line obituary:
Annamay Rose passed away
on June 15, 1973 at the age of 68.

Several months after she died
my dad bought the big home on Elmer Street
where she and her mother had lived for decades.

In each room the walls were lined
with her oil paintings,
large breathtaking images
of our village's quaint diverse life:
wheat fields,
Amish buggies,
Victorian homes,
Buckeye and Oak trees in every season,
Tommy Sadler's prized flower garden.

Everyone was stunned by such vibrant beauty,
shocked that Annamay Rose possessed such talent.

The discovery of her works of art
became the topic of conversation
at Curly Joe's local diner,
each person believing
they deserved to have a painting,
each saying that dead Annamay Rose
had been,
after all,
their best friend.

I Said Nothing

I wanted to tell them about the hummingbird.
How I cried when I saw it bathing,
how it gave me hope,
connected me to the Mystery,
to the One at the funeral they called God.

I wanted to tell them
I don't need to believe in their creed,
or accept Jesus into my heart
in order to be saved by God.
I am already saved, and have been
since I came out of my mother's womb.

I wanted to tell them
that for me God isn't
in the long sermon, altar call,
or loud praise music.
God is in the pink dogwood tree
dancing against the sanctuary window.

I wanted to tell them
I didn't believe what was being said
about God,
or dead Albert,
or heaven or hell.

I said nothing,
quietly left the funeral
grounded in my remembrance
of that moment with the hummingbird.

His Mother's Handkerchief

I was in the second grade
when I met my first love.
His name was Oscar Gutierrez,
son of a Mexican migrant worker.
He gave me his mother's handkerchief
on September 8, the birthday of the Blessed Mother.

The teacher took me aside to tell me
my mother would not approve of my liking him,
of his giving me gifts,
of our holding hands.

She was right. And I knew it.
My mom would not approve.
Neither would my dad, nor my minister,
and not my teacher.

But Oscar's mom approved.

Lying about where I was going,
I would often visit Oscar's mom
in the migrant camp.

I helped her cook and sew,
while she told me stories of
her native village people,
Oscar's hard life,
the many camps where they lived,
always being at the mercy of weather and crops.

She would ask me about my life,
something that seldom happened
in my own home.

I gave her back her handkerchief,
after she told me it belonged
to her dead mother.

One day, October 17 to be exact,
Oscar Gutierrez did not come to school.
His family was no longer in the camp.
I never saw him again.

His mother left me her handkerchief
in an envelope.
In her scrawl were the words,
Para quien lo ve:
"For one who sees."

Can You Spare A Dime?

He approached me on the corner of 5th and Alder.
Ma'am, can you spare me a dime?

Sorry, I only have one dollar, I said.

That will do.
Stay here and I'll be right back with your change.
Yeah. Sure, I said.

A few minutes later the burly, unshaven,
unkempt man returned with 90 cents.
Here's your change, Ma'am.

I treated him to black coffee
and a toasted wheat bagel with cheese.
He added four packets of sugar
and stirred his coffee nonstop.
I listened to some of his story.

I'm Richard. My friends call me Big R.
I'm a Vet, home from my third tour
of duty in Afghanistan.
I've had misfortunate times of late.
Don't know why exactly.
Maybe it is karma.
Maybe it is because I killed those people over there.
Had to, he said, as if fearful I was judging.

We went there to establish democracy,
to free the people.
Then we're told to kill them.
It never made sense to me.
But I did it.
And now I wonder about this karma thing.

I don't think it's karma, I said.
It's the system.
We don't know how to take care of the people
we send off with guns.

Tell me what you would like for your life, I asked.
I'd like to have my dignity back.

The conversation continued until
I needed to catch Bus 44 and head home.

Thanks for the dime, Ma'am.
Thanks for the change, I said.

Half Cup

Hey, it's Richard, he shouted,
as he ran across the street.
Do you remember me?

It was Richard, all right,
the homeless man I met some time ago
who hit me up for a dime, then a cup of coffee,
told me he was a vet of two wars, and when asked
what he wanted for his life,
he said he wanted his dignity back.

I owe you a cup of coffee, he said.
Can you spare some time? I'll be right back.

More curious than interested, I waited.
Richard returned with coffee and two cups.
Here, he said, as he poured a half cup.

"How are you, Richard?
It's been a long time since I've seen you."

I had a bit of good luck, Ma'am.
One morning I didn't wake up,
passed right out on the corner of 5th and Alder.
Police took me to the VA Hospital
where they said I had cancer.
I was so sick, in so much pain, I wanted to die.

"I'm sorry to hear about your cancer, Richard.
What was your bit of good luck?"

I didn't die.
I'm back on the streets.
This is my new spot, right here on Park Avenue.
I have a couple of new friends. I'm paying off my debts.

Next time we meet you can hit me up for
that half cup of coffee I still owe you.

He leaned his head back
and bellowed a hearty laugh.
I'm having a good day, Ma'am. I got to see you.

I thanked him for the coffee and walked on.
I didn't tell Richard
I now live in an upscale high-rise apartment
two blocks from where we were standing;
or that I was humbled being in
the presence of one so full of gratitude.

Her Son

I did not know her son.

I didn't even know her.

Still we wrapped our arms
around each other
like we were old friends.

He was the first Oregon soldier
to die in Iraq after the U.S. Occupation.

I went to his funeral.
It was the decent thing to do,
to pay my respects to someone
my tax dollars helped to kill.

The honor guard offered
the folded flag to the mother
saying her son was a hero.

When I shook her hand,
I said, "Hero or not,
he is still your son and he's dead."

That is when she hugged me.

That is when we both wept.

Saturday Is Funeral Day

Tafo is a small village
on the edge of Kunasi, Ghana

Tin shacks
Swollen bellies
Poverty so severe, so stark
You smell it creeping into you

With all the deaths that occur
Saturday is the designated funeral day

I am invited to join the funeral march

Black dress
Black head scarf
We line up
Right foot, left foot
Slowly swaying
To the rhythm of the drums

We stop
Long silence
The women begin to wail
I join them
Pounding our chests with our fists
Over and over
Until the fist on the chest
Becomes the drum beat to which we yell out
The names of loved ones
Now dead

Selma

I did not march from Selma to Montgomery in 1965.
I did not cross the Edmund Pettus Bridge, or walk
ten miles a day down Jefferson Davis Highway.

Instead I stood for days with others
in front of the White House, refusing to disperse,
pressuring Johnson to take action.

I was not brave enough to get on the bus.
I was only brave enough to stand and sing,
until a small group of us decided
to enter the Rotunda,
kneel in prayer, as our brother Martin did
on the Edmund Pettus Bridge the day before;

before he turned the group around
to head back to the church;
before white activist and minister James Reeb
was beaten to death;
before the decision was made to return
and cross the bridge,
walk the 54 miles to the State Capital,
an action leading to the passing
of the Voting Rights Act.

I was not brave enough to get on the bus,
just brave enough to keep kneeling
in prayer until arrested.

My friend Hal was brave.
He said he had to get on the bus for his own integrity,
so that his sermons were congruent with his actions.

Hal was not afraid.
His fear left him on January 27, 1945,
when he entered Auschwitz
to help liberate the innocent
men and women hardly breathing,
virtual skeletons still moving.

All fear left that day, Hal said,
when a man barely able to crawl,
touched his uniform pant leg
whispering **thank you**.
He wept every time he shared that story.

Hal decided on that January day
that he would give his
life to help liberate people from bondage,
including himself, his congregation, and now those
in Selma seeking the right to vote.

As I was praying in the Rotunda
hands behind my back, now cuffed,
I could hear Hal reminding me
that it's not really about being brave.
It's about seeking freedom from bondage.
About each of us responding to the call
on our heart, and taking the right next step.

Truth About Cammi

Cammi was getting up there in years.
She had many aches and pains,
but on her good days
she would bake sweet breads and cookies
for my daughter and me.

Cammi loved to tell stories about her younger days,
stories she referred to as "the yesteryears."

One day, while we were helping
clean her small home, Cammi became quite ill.
Two days later she quietly and peacefully died.

Her memorial service was held
in a small chapel at a local funeral home.
There were ten in attendance.
It was my daughter's first experience
with the rituals surrounding death.

The organist played what must have been
the slowest music in her repertoire.
We sang too many unfamiliar hymns.
After what seemed an eternity,
the minister began delivering Cammi's eulogy.

He spoke about all the things
Cammi had done for her church.
My daughter and I found his words interesting,
because to our knowledge she seldom,
if ever, attended church.
He spoke of her faithful devotion to her family,
which was puzzling, since her children were not
present, hadn't spoken to her in years.

The minister drummed on and on,
presenting one accolade after another.

Finally my six-year-old daughter said,
in a voice loud enough to make
the organist wince and the minister stop speaking,
"Who is he talking about, Mom?
That is not the Cammi I know!" And it wasn't.
My child's innocent interruption cut short the eulogy.
The service quickly ended.
The few gathered were dismissed.

On our way out of the chapel a feeble,
elderly gentleman stopped my daughter
and through tears asked,
"Young lady, could you tell me the stories
about the Cammi you know?
Cammi was my sister. I never really knew her."

We took the old man to a nearby bakery
and held our own lengthy memorial service.
We shared our favorite stories of "the yesteryears,"
as we treated ourselves to the baked goods
we knew Cammi would have enjoyed.

Years have passed, and my daughter and I
have often laughed about that day,
about the look on the minister's face
as he heard a young child speak truth,
about Cammi's brother becoming our friend,
about how only a few years after she died
we, at his request, held his memorial service
in the bakery.

Out of Darkness

No one noticed she took the garbage out at 4 a.m.,
right before she started baking pies and breads
that needed to be finished by the time
her small bakery opened at 8.

Her pies and breads would all be sold by 10:30 a.m.
when she closed the shop
and began creating made-to-order cakes
that customers needed to pick up by 3 p.m.

No one noticed that at 3:30
she again took out the garbage and started
preparations for her evening class
on how to decorate cakes for the holidays.

No one noticed her nonstop humming
the lightness in her steps
twinkle in her eyes
unending smile on her face.

She was the only one who noticed
she had found her own way
out of the darkness and depression
that had plagued her life for twenty years.

Petals for Rosemary

It was a long drive to the cemetery.
I rode in the car
with Rosemary's mom.

We gathered in a circle
around her grave.
Rosemary was only eighteen.
We were the same age,
shared the same clothes,
boyfriends, secrets.
She was my best friend.
The first person I had seen dead.

Rosemary's mother was hysterical.
My mother was home in bed,
her way of dealing with pain.
I was numb.

Someone played the flute.
Someone sang.
Others whispered about how
Rosemary ended up in the pine box
now covered with violet and blue
flowers.

"Why?" sobbed her mother,
over and over again. "Why?"

"Death has no sting," began the
minister. "She is in God's hands.
We are here to celebrate a life
so courageously lived.
We are here to offer forgiveness to the
one who caused her such harm."

My knees started to shake.
"Shut the fuck up!" I screamed.

The startled minister could only
whisper, "Amen."

Silence hung in the air.
One by one the mourners left,
except for Rosemary's mom and me.
We wrapped arms around each other as
the bruised, raped, battered body of my best friend
was lowered into the ground.

We stood for hours tossing rose petals on the grave,
accompanied only by the tears of the gravedigger.

Step 12 – Having had a spiritual awakening as the result of these steps, we tried to carry this message to others, and to practice these principles in all our affairs.

Choose Between This Or That

How did you quit drinking? he asked.
    I stopped putting alcohol in my mouth.
Was that hard? Did you look like a drunk?
    It was hell. Tell me what a drunk looks like.
Do you think you are cured? How do you know
you won't drink again?
    I'm not cured, and I don't know if I'll drink
    again. I only know that today,
    and 22 years' worth of days, I haven't.
Do you think God healed you?
    No, I think I quit drinking
    and in the process God was there.
I've lost so much. I wonder if there is any hope
I could quit.
    All depends on what you are willing to do
    to live life sober.

This was my second conversation with Glen,
right after the one about his dad dying
and his wife leaving.
A friend had asked me to meet with Glen,
saying he was in a desperate place, and he was.

I spelled out a list of things that helped me
stay clean and sober one day at a time;
how every step forward was costly and challenging.
How we each have to find our own way,
but regardless of the way, the goal is the same –
   no alcohol, none, ever.

I told him every minute of every day we have
choices, not just about drinking,
but about everything.

On my way home I thought about other addictions
I had given up, about addictions I still have.
I thought about the high price one pays
for either bondage or liberation.

Brown Paper Bag

He had many brown paper bags,
held the illusion
no one knew what was in them.

Everyone knew.
I knew, and so did his wife,
and daughters,
and granddaughters.
No one talked about it.

The brown paper bags
carried bottles of whiskey,
magazines of nude women
in poses disturbing and confusing.

As an eight-year-old
I became anxious whenever
I saw the brown paper bags,
held fear of the man carrying them.

Even at this young age
I knew not to get too close,
never to be alone, to always lock
the bathroom and bedroom doors behind me.

At a family gathering
long after the man and his wife had died,
I shared how frightened and uneasy I was
by the man with the brown paper bags.

What I shared made three women cry.
I knew then
the story behind their tears,
the reason for my childhood uneasiness.

The man,
a sexual predator,
a real son-of-a-bitch
was my grandfather.

The Poet of Easter Sunrise

Easter morning, trees blooming
Sun rising behind Mount Hood
I come to Mt. Tabor early
To take pictures before sunrise service

I snap a photo of her getting out of the taxi
Thin, bent over, unkempt
Big heavy Bible under her arm
Wearing an old long khaki coat
Tattered black winter hat
She looks fragile, says her name is Priscilla
Later says it is Debra
She comes every year for the sunrise service
Doesn't know which church will be there
Doesn't care

I hold her arm
As we walk down a hill to the amphitheater
I ask about her life, where she lives
What she does during her days
Says she writes songs and poetry
I ask if she has any with her
She does – in her head

She recites a lengthy poem
about the meaning of Easter
It isn't about back then but about right now
About the rising and falling
The death and life I experience everyday

She recites another about Martin Luther King, Jr.
A prophet, a black man, a teacher preaching injustice
anywhere is a threat to justice everywhere
Don't judge by the color of one's skin
But by the content of one's words, one's character

Says she sent both poems to the local newspaper
Was told they were too controversial to print

The sunrise service begins
The minister asks what signs we see of resurrection
Priscilla Debra shouted *baptism*
She seems bored with the service
Asks for a ride to her church nearby

Walking back up the hill
She sings songs she has written
About the meaning of Hallelujah

Jesus shows up in our lives today
Though we seldom recognize him
He doesn't look like the church photos
He isn't always a him
He comes to remind us what we forget
About the meaning of love
How we should treat one another
That there is nothing to prove and nothing to protect
We are who we are and that's enough
Success is decided not by the amount of money
But by the quality of our service to those who have little
Resurrection happens when we let go
Of who we are not... and what we don't need

We drive down the steep hills
Around the corner to her church
She does not want me to walk her up
The old rickety wood plank to the door
I will go it alone, she says

I can't prove this
But while I was with her I thought
Priscilla Debra was Jesus

Life Unlived

I watched as she slowly brushed back
her thick locks of white hair

She was beautiful
though she did not know it

Just as she did not know
she was wise
gifted with words
creative with her hands

What she knew was
she was unfulfilled
unhappy
imprisoned in her depression

What I knew was
I loved her
found it difficult to be around her
feared inheriting the unlived life

School of Death

I was five when she died.

She, a long-haired
calico barn cat
named Tabby.

I killed her.

Not on purpose.
Not because I wanted harm or
death to come to her.
I didn't even know what death was;
I had never witnessed it.

I killed her because she fell down a deep hole
I had uncovered.

Grandfather had dug the hole for a fence post to
keep his animals from traveling
across the farmland, and doing more damage
to disgruntled Mr. Humphrey's yard.

Grandfather had massive hands,
was tall, solid, strong,
half Iroquois, half something else.
I felt troubled around him sometimes,
but liked watching him work.

When he took a break to fetch his whiskey,
he covered the hole,
giving me strict instructions
to not go near or uncover it.

I did both about the time Tabby showed up.
She fell in the hole.

I heard a dull thumping sound.
I was terrified.
I yelled down at her until my throat hurt.

No sound.
No meow.

I knew then that silence
was one component of death.

Grandfather came back,
put the fence post in the hole,
filled the hole with dirt.

I didn't tell him about Tabby.
I did not tell anyone.

I had nightmares instead.

Prison Prophet:
A True Story of Redemption

They hired me to work with you.
You were charged with
distribution of a narcotic.
I went with you to the detox unit.
You urinated on my shoe,
threw up on my coat,
and I set out to save you.

"Fuck off, white bitch," you screamed.
I wiped up your mess and silently said,
"Shut up, black woman, just shut up."

I was given orders to stay with you
make sure you didn't escape.
An unlikely possibility.
You couldn't walk,
couldn't stand up, wouldn't eat.
Your mind was fogged.
All you could say was,
"Get fucked, white bitch, get fucked."

I sat with you,
held your hand,
whispered prayers in your ear,
heard your screams,
watched you give birth.
You cried.
I cried.
Your baby cried.

You became hysterical.
"White bitch, don't take my baby.

That's my baby."
They gave me your baby – a girl,
4 lbs. 2 oz.,
born addicted,
born traumatized.

I carried your baby to the trauma unit.
From behind locked doors
and down hallways
I heard your screams, curses, threats.
I felt your hate, fear, sadness,
your desperation.

You lived.
The baby lived.
I lived.
But all three of us
were having trouble with life.

I petitioned the court to terminate
your parental rights.
The baby, now four months old,
labeled "fetal drug baby, slow,
possible retardation; future: suspect"
was adopted by a young black family.

Months later your file landed on my desk.
It read:
Sentenced to prison
Ten to twelve
Housed in cell-block D
Treatment Counselor is...

Oh Damn. Not me.
Oh God, please, not me.

Our time together
was Tuesday 8 a.m., every other week.
And slowly, over weeks, months, years,
I heard your story,
felt your pain,
held your tears in my heart,
carried your wounds in my soul.

You were raped at age five,
serviced out to mother's friends.
Your body paid her bills.
Left at grandmother's at age nine,
finally a place to feel safe,
a place to call home.
Then Grandma died and you were
placed – displaced –
into a white Christian family,
used by the dad for gratification,
showed off by the mom to
prove her good works.

Eventually you stopped calling me
"white bitch," and gave me
the name Ms. Esther.
I stopped silently saying,
"Shut up, black woman,"
and called you Kathy.

In prison
you completed high school,
wrote beautiful poetry,
composed songs,
gave voice to the pain,
and spoke from a depth seldom heard.

Your prophetic utterances about the truth of life
shook me to the core.
On the outside of your file I wrote,
Prophet – The Prison Prophet.

You were released.
We kept in touch.
I married.
You married.
You had another baby.
I raised mine.
You traveled far to pay me a visit,
to say thanks –
for what, I am not yet sure.
You offered me forgiveness –
for what, you could not say.
You looked tough, fragile,
smelled of death.

I never saw you again.
My letters to you were returned,
stamped "Occupant Unknown."

But I know who you are.
You are Kathy – The Prison Prophet.

Full Circle

I saw her often
Standing on the stony shore
Of the river bank
Long grey hair
Long black coat
Bent over
Thoughtfully placing rocks
One on top of the other

A year into watching her
And feeling brave
I asked her who she was
What she was doing

One day, she said
You will know
And went back to placing rocks
I went back to watching

Decades later
I thought I saw her
On a different river bank
Building altars to her God
She looked a lot like me

Night Ritual

Almost every evening
When my daughter was young
I'd crawl into her bed
Snuggle beneath the covers

She would say
Tell me a story
Sometimes she would add
Make it really good or
Make it very scary or
Tell the one you told last night
The one about the big fluffy brown dog with the sloppy
kisses

Even when friends were over
We'd honor our ritual
Bed
Story
Two stories when friends were there
Three stories if she was sick

One evening when I was in bed with a fever and cold
My daughter crawled under my sheets
And said
Let me tell you a story
Once upon a time there was
A big fluffy brown dog...

Nothing Perfect

She secured the rope to the basement beam,
put the noose around her neck,
kicked the chair from under her feet.
Her suicide was complete.

Several hours later
Anna's mother found her daughter hanging.
She didn't weep or talk about it.
She busied herself with
choosing the perfect casket,
perfect wake, perfect memorial service.

Everything turned out perfect
except, Anna was dead.

I spoke at the funeral.
I talked not about Anna,
and not to her mom,
still desperately clinging to false memories
of a perfect daughter.

I spoke to her young friends
about the myth of courage
and the downside of the rope.

A Simple Meal

Calcutta, India

Working in Mother Teresa's
Home for the Destitute and Dying
I was given the task of feeding Isa

We didn't know her real name
One of the Sisters brought her in from the streets
We called her Isa because a volunteer thought
she looked like her Aunt Isa May

I tried to feed Isa protein porridge
She didn't want it, kept spitting it out

Out of frustration
I went to the chapel in the adjoining room
To do a forbidden thing
I took a wafer off the Communion table
And brought it back to Isa
saying in a soft no-nonsense voice

This is the body of Christ
Now take
And eat

Isa stuck out her tongue and I placed the wafer on it
It took time but eventually she was able to swallow
Then she looked up at me
and whispered in perfect English

Do you have any wine?

Cot 44

I gave her a drink,
or at least I tried.
I didn't know she could not swallow,
that she was in this Home for
the Destitute and Dying in Calcutta, India,
because she might die today
or maybe tomorrow.

She wasn't here yesterday
when I came to volunteer.
The Sisters found her on
the streets this morning,
as they made their rounds
in the neighborhood
choosing who gets to die
lying on clean sheets
surrounded by those who care.

No one knew her name,
just that she was on cot 44,
and would be there until she died.

I put down the cup of water
and sat beside her.
I stared at her for a long time.
Just stared, trying to absorb what I knew:
I would be the one,
in Mother Teresa's words,
who would "love her into heaven."

I had never loved anyone into heaven.
I did not know how to do that.

I decided to prepare her body.
I poured the cup of water into a shallow bowl,
soaked a clean cloth,
and began to wash her face,
her arms,
her legs,
her feet.

I laid her hands on her belly,
placed mine over hers, and began to sing, in English
a song I learned as a child,
"Jesus loves me, this I know…"

Moisture formed in her eyes.

Did she know what I was singing?
Did she, this Hindu woman,
know she was loved?

Hours passed.
Many hours.
The Sisters brought me bread.

Early in the morning on the third day
she stopped breathing.

I was mesmerized by the angelic look on her face,
surprised at the peaceful pulse of my heart.

Two young volunteers
wrapped her in a shroud,
carried her on the cot to wherever
they carry the dead.

I moved on to cot 45.

Ted and Barney

Ted loved more than anything else
his cows and his dog, Barney.

Seven months before Ted died
Barney showed up at the front door
and barked until he was let in.

They bonded immediately.

Ted made half-hearted attempts
to find Barney's owner.
When he couldn't, Barney stayed.

The two became inseparable.

Hours before Ted died,
Barney came in from the back porch,
stood in the archway of the living room,
got down on his belly,
and scooted across the floor
to the hospice bed.

He jumped gently on the bed and
slowly, softly,
ever so tenderly,
licked Ted's face.

Off the bed,
back on his belly,
he scooted to the kitchen
and out the back door.
Later that evening Ted died.
Barney, his work now complete,
was nowhere to be found.

Waiting for the Words

When Mother became terminally ill,
I made a monthly pilgrimage to be with her.
To sit, hold her hand,
do her laundry,
ponder with her the question of "why?"

On the last day, of our last visit,
I told her goodbye, thanked her
for being my mother,
told her I loved her.

I longed to hear her say those words.

She never did.

I spent years believing
her inability to say "I love you" was about me.

It wasn't.

The Covenant

Fifteen years ago we made a covenant
that none of our own would die alone.

I listened as three men reflected on their experience
of the past five weeks accompanying their friend
Samuel, *through the gate to the other side.*

Jeffery Jonathan spoke on behalf of the others.

Samuel was never by himself.
We took turns singing, chanting, feeding, bathing him.
He died the way he came in, beloved and loved.

"What led you to make such a covenant?" I asked.
"And who are your own?"

Our own, said Jeffery Jonathan,
is any man who has suffered
discrimination, injustice or emotional harm
because of his sexual orientation.
A group of us made the covenant
when Leonard died of AIDS fifteen years ago.
The hospital would not admit him.
The foster home would not let us visit,
because of their fear of whatever we represented.
So we literally picked Leonard up
and brought him to Dan's home,
attended to his every need
until he died six days later.

It was during Leonard's memorial service
that we made a covenant of solidarity –
that not one of our own would die alone.
Since that day of laments for Leonard,
eighty-three men have died in our arms.

Take Good Notes

The phone rang at 6:05 a.m.
The news was not good:
aggressive cancer – terminal.

I booked a flight for the next afternoon,
quickly packed the suitcase
along with the black dress,
knowing I would be with her
until she died.

My sister was director of hospice
in a large assisted-living facility.

She once trained staff and volunteers
to care for the dying,
wrote and published articles on end-of-life,
facilitated grief groups,
was recognized for her skills and work
in compassionate care.

She greeted me at the door with,
I haven't long, so let's get busy.
Follow me around with your pen and paper.
I am the one the next article needs to be about.
Take good notes.

So I did.
I wrote her words,
her instructions,
her experiences of the last stage of her journey.

Toward the end, her children asked
if she was scared.
Not scared, she said.
Just curious.

"What will happen to you," they inquired.
I'll just evaporate back into God.

Did you write that down, Sister?
I'll just evaporate.

I was with her for six weeks
taking notes.

She held court like a queen,
directing her death
with confidence, wisdom, grace.

I took my notes home,
and as instructed,
wrote the article about her dying process
for her friends and for hospice.

All the while wondering
what she knows and sees
from her evaporated state.

Rise and Fall

I watched her chest
rise
slowly
fall
slowly
Over and over
until it stopped.

Days before the rising and falling stopped
I asked what she thought would happen
when she died.

Nothing much.
Nothing but to evaporate back into God.
There is little difference
between here and there,
except you won't see me.
Once I am with the ancestors,
you will only hear me breathe.

And so
on that day,
and every day since
the rising and falling stopped,
I have been listening…
listening…

The Gift

A large statue of the Servant Christ
sits in front of Christ House,
a recovery facility for the homeless.

The impressive bronze statue
crafted by American artist Jimilu Mason
portrays Jesus kneeling with his hands open
ready to receive.

One day Jonah
was picking up the trash around the Servant Christ:
old discarded containers, half-eaten sandwiches,
candy wrappers, notes with appointment dates.

His bag of trash was getting full
when he saw in the hands of the Servant Christ
a brown paper bag
with the top of a whiskey bottle sticking out.

Jonah started to pick up the bag
when a man dressed in old tattered clothes
and dirty unkempt hair shouted,
"Leave that bag alone mister!
It's a gift to my Jesus!
That's my Jesus you are messing with!"

Jonah carefully put the bag back into the hands
of the Servant Christ and said to the man,
"Well...he is also my Jesus."

Without a pause the man responded,
"I gave him my last drop of whiskey.
What about you?
What did you give him?"

We don't always get to choose who we are given.
But we can count on this – people come
into our lives at just the right time to teach us
the lessons we still need to learn. Gordon Cosby

Thursday Meet Up

I met Billy at 9 a.m. on the corner of 10th and Yamhill
in front of the library just like we agreed to do
before I moved out of his neighborhood.

I didn't actually think he would show.
Being a street vender, and at times homeless,
I knew his plans could easily change.

He arrived early, thirty minutes before I did,
said he wanted to get us a good spot.
Getting a good spot on a street corner
was a new concept for me.

I brought coffee and tea.
He liked his coffee strong, three sugars,
two hits of cream.

Billy's mother, I found out,
gave him up for adoption.
Well actually, she just disappeared one day
when he was with his grandma.
Grandma died when he was three,
that's when he was adopted "more or less" he said,
by Aunt Mildred, a woman who didn't like children,
and specifically didn't like Billy.
I was too black for her.

As I started to pick up our papers,
Billy said, *We will meet here at 9 a.m.*
next Thursday, just like we will do every Thursday.
You can be the mother I never had.

"How old are you Billy?" I asked.
Old enough to be a good son. How old are you?
"Old enough to be a good mom."

Billy laughed, held onto my arm,
walked me to the bus stop,
thanked me for the coffee and our time together.

On the way home I thought about Gordon's words,
knowing that Billy and I have been given.

Black and White

I met Billy where I meet him every Thursday,
in front of the library.
This Thursday it was pouring rain.
I suggested we go to the nearby
coffee shop and stay dry.

I can't go, he said,
it wouldn't be right to go there with you.
People would be upset. Their words could hurt you.
It could harm my business if people see a black man
who sells newspapers for the homeless
sitting in that establishment
with a white woman your age.
They would say I was 'pimping' you,
trying to take your money.

Now
heavy at heart
black homeless reality
white middle class privilege.

Two Sides of the Door

We were on opposite sides of the door

So you could not know
The agony of hearing
The sound of metal clanging shut behind you
The tears that fell
The sounds of weeping and wailing
Of a mother's breaking heart

You could not know of such things
Just as I could not know
What it felt like to walk
Down a long corridor to an empty room
Where they promised
You could do no harm

Go Home

Once while working with Mother Teresa,
I asked what I should do
to heal the sick and feed the poor.

Go home, she said, *and do acts of loving-kindness
to those in your family.*

Wise people can name what is true.
I knew that going home and loving my family
would be my hardest work to date.

Recently separated from my husband,
daughter soon leaving to chart her journey,
and I, being fresh into recovery, knew
life ahead would be challenging.

A bit deflated from Mother Teresa's instructions,
I sat on a cement bench.
A young patient barely able to walk
came and sat next to me.
She spoke only Hindi, I spoke only English.
We sat in silence holding hands
for over two hours.

On my way to serve lunch
I apologized to Mother Teresa
for not doing any work that morning.
She responded, *You were practicing being present,
our most important work.*

Back home, I thought a lot about my time
with this saint of the streets of Calcutta
how she owned only two saris and a bucket,
and seemed so centered, so at peace,
so clear about her work and mission.

Even today, decades later,
I can hear her voice, her words,
Go home, be present, do acts of loving-kindness,
and know this to be my right and endless work.

Two Sides of the Door

Contact Esther Elizabeth at
estherwelizabeth@gmail.com
for permission to use any portion
of this book

Made in the USA
San Bernardino, CA
15 May 2016